TEXT COPYRIGHT © BLACK STARS PRESS

All rights reserved. No part of this planner may be reproduced in any form without permission in writing from the publisher except in the case of brief quotations embodied in critical articles or reviews.

LEGAL & DISCLAIMER

This planner and its contents are not a legally binding document. Users should consult an attorney to complete their will and other legally binding documents, arrangements, and miscellanea pertaining to his or her last wishes, funerary arrangements, and all incapacitation or postmortem matters. The author[s], publisher[s], editor[s], and all parties associated with the creation and distribution of this planner are, under no circumstances, responsible for any damages arising out of or in connection with the purchase and use of this planner, including but not limited to: identity theft, revelation of sensitive information including passwords and identity numbers, incomplete or misleading post-mortem or incapacitated instructions, or the failure to store, complete, find, or utilize this planner or the information therein on the part of the owner, his or her family members, caregivers, lawyers, or other parties. Owners and users are responsible for the safekeeping of this planner and any sensitive information it may contain upon completion or partial completion. This planner does not claim to be a complete resource for postmortem or incapacitation affairs and communication, nor a complete personal record. Users agree to use this planner as nothing more than a thorough yet possibly incomplete guide for recording personal information that may be relevant after death or incapacitation.

TABLE OF CONTENTS

Introduction 5

Part One: Basic Information 8

Part Two: Documents You Will Need; Important Contacts 38

Part Three: Finances 50

Part Four: Property 70

Part Five: Recurring Bills or Autopays 106

Part Six: Odds and Ends 114

Part Seven: Parting Words 136

SORRY
FOR YOUR LOSS

IT'S ME

TO THE OWNER OF THIS PLANNER:

Losing a loved one is never easy; most of us would prefer not to think about it at all, including the sad and confusing details of our own passing. Planning ahead is crucial, though, as it can not only ease that fear of the unknown for us, but also provide our loved ones with a sense of control and measure of peace after we pass, or if we should lose our ability to clearly communicate our needs and wishes.

This planner is designed to be as comprehensive and helpful as possible; as such, you may find categories or sections that do not apply to you. Feel free to skip these, or return to them as needed in the future.

For the sections that are applicable, be as detailed as possible; you can even make a note like "continued at the back of this book" (where you'll find several lined, blank pages for your use) should you run out of room in any particular area.

Obviously, this is a time-intensive project — so don't feel pressured to fill it all out at once! You'll likely have to research quite a bit: contact numbers, policy numbers, etc. If it takes a few weeks or even months, that's fine. You can also ask a trusted loved one to help you fill it out.

Because this planner will have to be updated regularly and kept as consistent with your living will as possible, we recommend filling it out in pencil or erasable pen for easy changes. This will save your loved ones time, money, confusion, and anguish; discrepancies between a document such as this and a legally binding one can cause headaches (and heartache) for families and friends, so try to update and compare the two frequently.

Setting a reminder in your phone or writing reminders on a calendar can help: semi-annual read-throughs, to make sure all applicable information is filled out and correct, will ensure this planner stays as current as possible.

It's important to note that this planner is not a legal document. While it can help your loved ones and beneficiaries understand your wishes and their roles better, what's written here is not legally binding; you still need to draft a valid will.

This planner will, when completed, contain highly sensitive information—so be sure to store it in a safe and secure place, such as a combination safe or deposit box. Tell your lawyer and/or family members where to find the book, should you pass suddenly or be unable to communicate.

TO THE LOVED ONES READING THIS PLANNER:

We hope this planner eases some of the confusion that comes with the death or incapacitation of a loved one. We've organized it to start with the most basic information you'll need, moving into more in-depth topics—but feel free to skip ahead to any relevant section, at any time. We wish you peace and comfort in this time of heartache and grief. Please know that your loved one cared for you deeply, and thus wanted his or her passing to go as smoothly as possible for those they left behind.

The rest of this book will be written for you, from the viewpoint of your loved one (not only in the information they filled out themselves, but the published portions, as well) unless otherwise noted. Consult the introductions at the start of each section if you encounter anything in need of clarification.

PART ONE

BASIC INFORMATION

This section encompasses all the basic information you could possibly need to know, from my legal name (which, ideally, you already know!), all the way to my dependents and pets. You'll also find my personal wishes and a brief overview of what I would like to happen upon my passing.

BASIC INFORMATION

Name:
....

Relevant Nicknames and Variations:
....

....

Maiden Name, if applicable:
....

Most Recent Physical Address:
....

....

PO Box Number and Location of Key, if applicable:
....

....

Phone Number(s): Mobile .... Home ....

Office .... Fax ....

Social Security Number (SSN Card's location can be found in Part Two):
....

....

Birthplace Information:
....

....

Birth Certificate Number: (Birth Certificate location can be found in Part Two):
....

....

Business License Location:
....

....

....

FAMILY INFORMATION

In this section, you'll find the names of family members and information on current and previous marriages, as well as religious and occupational information.
TO THE OWNER OF THIS PLANNER: please indicate beside each name if the person is now deceased.

Marital Status:
....

Name of Spouse, if applicable:
....

Names of Children or Stepchildren, if applicable:

....

....

....

Names of Grandchildren, if applicable:

....

....

....

Previous Marriages? (Circle Yes or No)   Yes   No

If yes, list former spouses' names and date ranges of marriages:

....

....

Names of Siblings:

....

....

10

....

....

....

Father's Name and Birthplace: ....

....

....

Mother's Name (Maiden) and Birthplace: ....

....

MISCELLANEOUS BASIC INFORMATION

Job Title and Place of Employment: ....

....

....

....

....

Citizenship Status: ....

Religion and place of worship: ....

....

Military Service History and Important Details: ....

....

NOTES

MY PETS

The name(s) of my pet or pets, and what kind of animal they are:

....

....

....

....

....

....

How old each pet is:

....

....

....

....

Each pets' license or ID information:

....

....

....

....

....

....

Who Will Take Care of My Pet(s) When I'm Gone or Unable to Do So Myself:
....

His or Her Phone Number:
....

Should The Person Above Be Unable to Care for Pet(s), Please Contact this Person as a Potential Replacement:
....

....

His or Her Phone Number:
....

Veterinarian Name and Number:
....

HOW TO CARE FOR MY PET(S)

My pet likes :
....

....

....

My pet dislikes:
....

....

....

Things that frighten or upset my pet are...

....

....

Dietary restrictions or allergies:

....

....

Medical issues:

....

....

One special thing I did with or for my pet that I would like continued is....

....

....

....

My pet likes:

....

....

My pet dislikes:

....

....

....

Things that frighten or upset my pet are...
....

....

....

Dietary restrictions or allergies:
....

....

....

Medical issues:
....

....

....

One special thing I did with or for my pet that I would like continued is....
....

....

....

....

My pet likes:
....

....

....

Things that frighten or upset my pet are...

....

....

Dietary restrictions or allergies:

....

....

Medical issues:

....

....

One special thing I did with or for my pet that I would like continued is.....

....

....

....

My pet likes:

....

....

My pet dislikes:

....

....

....

Things that frighten or upset my pet are...
....

....

....

Dietary restrictions or allergies:
....

....

....

Medical issues:
....

....

....

One special thing I did with or for my pet that I would like continued is....
....

....

....

My pet likes:
....

....

....

Things that frighten or upset my pet are…

....

....

....

Dietary restrictions or allergies:

....

....

....

Medical issues:

....

....

One special thing I did with or for my pet that I would like continued is….

....

....

....

Notes:

....

....

....

....

WHEN I PASS.

Please consult this section at the time of my passing to know who to contact first. You'll need to request copies of my death certificate from my doctor for legal and insurance purposes. A funeral director can also provide these.

TO THE OWNER OF THIS PLANNER: Write down anyone you want to be contacted immediately upon your death or incapacitation, even if they may be the person who first reads this planner/the one contacting people upon your passing. This ensures no one on your First Contacts list gets skipped.

WHO TO CONTACT FIRST

Name: ....

Relationship: ....

Phone Number: ....

....

Name: ....

Relationship: ....

Phone Number: ....

....

Name: ....

Relationship: ....

Phone Number: ....

....

Name: ....

Relationship: ....

Phone Number: ....

....

Name: ....

Relationship: ....

Phone Number: ....

Name: ....

Relationship: ....

Phone Number: ....

....

Name: ....

Relationship: ....

Phone Number: ....

....

Name: ....

Relationship: ....

Phone Number: ....

....

Name: ....

Relationship: ....

Phone Number: ....

....

Employer: ....

Name of Supervisor/HR Head or other Relevant Party: ....

Phone Number: ....

....

MY FUNERAL ARRANGEMENTS

Who to Contact: ....

Preferred or Prearranged Funeral Home: ....

Funeral Insurance? Circle one: Yes   No ....

Policy Number and Company: ....

....

(Circle one):   Burial   or   Cremation ....

If "Burial" is Circled, Please Specify Burial site/Cemetery: ....

....

Grave Marker Already Ordered (Circle one):   Yes   No ....

If Yes, Where Is It Located? ....

....

....

Desired Epitaph, if any: ....

....

....

....

....

....

If "Cremation" is Circled: will ashes be scattered or kept, or left at the discretion of loved ones?

....

....

....

How Many People Will Receive Ashes:

Names:

....

....

....

If ashes will be scattered, where and when I would like this to occur is....

....

....

....

I would prefer a... (Circle one):   Celebration of life   Traditional funeral

(Note: the main difference between a celebration of life and a traditional funeral is that the body is present, cremated or in a casket, at the funeral; it has already been cremated/scattered/buried at a celebration of life, which has less formality. If you are unsure about the type of service you want, consult a funeral director, or ask your family for their input on how they would like to grieve your loss, say goodbye, and honor your memory. Every family is different!)

Guests I would like to attend my funeral:

....

....

....

....

....

....

....

Are there any words I would like my funeral guests to hear, or stories I'd like shared? Poems or bible verses I would like to read? If you have a preferred eulogist (or several), make note of that here, as well.

....

....

....

....

....

....

Other notes on my funerary arrangements:

....

....

....

....

OBITUARY

Information I'd like included in my obituary (surviving family members, lifetime achievements, where people can send flowers or "in lieu of" donations, etc.):

....

....

....

....

....

....

....

....

....

....

....

....

....

....

....

....

....

....

WHAT BENEFICIARIES CAN EXPECT

This section includes the names and numbers of my beneficiaries, as well as the first information they will need to know when I pass.

BENEFICIARIES:

Name: ....

Relationship: ....

Phone Number: ....

....

Name: ....

Relationship: ....

Phone Number: ....

....

Name: ....

Relationship: ....

Phone Number: ....

Document Information and Location(s) my Beneficiaries will Need to Know: ....

....

....

....

....

INSURANCE POLICIES

What kind of policy is it?

Beneficiary for this Policy:

Account Number:

Company:

Company Contact Information:

Amount:

Where to Find the Documents for this Policy:

Misc. Notes on this Policy:

What kind of policy is it?

Beneficiary for this Policy:

Account Number:

Company:

Company Contact Information:

Amount:

Where to Find the Documents for this Policy:

Misc. Notes on this Policy:

What kind of policy is it? ....

Beneficiary for this Policy: ....

Account Number: ....

Company: ....

Company Contact Information: ....

Amount: ....

Where to Find the Documents for this Policy: ....

Misc. Notes on this Policy: ....

....

....

What kind of policy is it? ....

Beneficiary for this Policy: ....

Account Number: ....

Company: ....

Company Contact Information: ....

Amount: ....

Where to Find the Documents for this Policy: ....

Misc. Notes on this Policy: ....

....

....

SOCIAL SECURITY INFORMATION

Name and account number: ....

Company contact: ....

Where to find the documents for this policy: ....

....

....

....

Misc. Notes on this Policy: ....

....

....

RETIREMENT ACCOUNTS

Name and account number: ....

....

Company contact: ....

Where to Find the Documents for this Policy: ....

....

....

Misc. Notes on this Policy: ....

....

....

Name and account number:

....

....

Company contact: ....

Where to Find the Documents for this Policy: ....

....

....

Misc. Notes on this Policy: ....

....

....

....

Name and account number: ....

....

Company contact: ....

Where to Find the Documents for this Policy: ....

....

....

Misc. Notes on this Policy: ....

....

....

....

BENEFITS FROM EMPLOYER

Name and account number:
....

Company contact:
....

Where to find the documents for this policy:
....

....

....

....

Misc. Notes on this Policy:
....

....

....

VETERAN BENEFITS

Name and account number:
....

....

Company contact:
....

Where to Find the Documents for this Policy:
....

....

....

Misc. Notes on this Policy:
....

....

....

Misc. Notes on this section, or other key information my beneficiaries will need to know first:

....

....

....

....

....

....

....

....

....

....

....

....

....

....

....

....

....

....

MY PERSONAL WISHES.

In this section, you will find any remaining descriptions of my funerary services, pet or home care, and miscellaneous affairs I would like handled in a specific way.

TO THE OWNER OF THIS PLANNER: if there are any "must have" wishes you'd like to take precedence over others, please indicate these with an asterisk so your loved ones know which mattered most to you. If there's anything you'd like to happen a certain way, but don't mind if it doesn't, indicate this as well (for example: "I would like my ashes scattered in the aforementioned location, but funds permitting; the following places are also fine, should that be more convenient"). You can also make notes of who you'd like to speak at your funeral service, any poems or religious texts you'd like read, and other wishes not yet noted in Part 1.

....

....

....

....

....

....

....

....

....

....

....

....

....

....

PART TWO

DOCUMENTS YOU WILL NEED AND IMPORTANT CONTACTS

In this part of the planner, you'll find descriptions of personal and important documents you'll need in the coming days, weeks, and months. I've also included the location of each document and the most important information from each item.

Key contacts regarding my medical and legal needs are also included.

MY WILL

Where you can find my will:
....

....

....

How many hard copies exist:
....

How many electronic copies exist, and where they are located:
....

....

....

ID AND OTHER IMPORTANT DOCUMENTS

Birth certificate location:
....

....

Driver's License number:
....

Where you can find it:
....

....

Passport number:
....

Where you can find it:
....

....

....

Marriage certificate location:

....

If applicable - divorce papers location:

....

Address book? Circle one: Yes   No

Location:

....

INSURANCE DOCUMENTS

Life insurance

Agent Name:

Company Name:

Phone Number:

Where to find the document for this policy:

....

Health insurance

Agent Name:

Company Name:

Phone Number:

Where to find the document for this policy:

....

Medicare or Medicaid

Is this supplementary insurance? Circle one: Yes   No
....

Account Number:
....

Where to find my insurance card(s):
....

....

Dental insurance

Insurer name and contact:
....

Account number:
....

....

Vision insurance

Insurer name and contact:
....

Account number:
....

....

Homeowner's insurance

Agent Name:
....

Company Name:
....

Phone Number:
....

Where to find the document for this policy:
....

....

....

Rental insurance

Agent Name: ....

Company Name: ....

Phone Number: ....

Where to find the document for this policy: ....

....

....

Storage Unit insurance

Agent Name: ....

Company Name: ....

Phone Number: ....

Where to find the document for this policy: ....

....

....

Auto insurance

Agent Name: ....

Company Name: ....

Phone Number: ....

....

....

Misc. insurance

Type of insurance: ....

Company Name: ....

Phone Number: ....

Where to find the document for this policy: ....

....

....

Misc. insurance

Type of insurance: ....

Company Name: ....

Phone Number: ....

Where to find the document for this policy: ....

....

....

Misc. Notes regarding insurance policies (Electronic information, such as computer passwords and social media log-ins, is located in Part Six: Odds and Ends):

....

....

....

....

....

Misc. Notes Regarding Documents You May Need

BASIC MEDICAL INFORMATION

Medical Contacts

Healthcare power of attorney agent: ....

Their phone number: ....

Relationship to me: ....

Where you can find the document for this: ....

....

....

DNR (Do Not Resuscitate) Order? Circle one: Yes   No

Location of this DNR Order, if you circled Yes: ....

....

....

Organ donor? Circle one: Yes   No

Document/confirmation of decision, if "Yes": ....

....

....

Basic Medical Information

Allergies and severity of reactions: ....

....

....

Blood type: ....

Other medical conditions: ....

....

....

....

....

....

Health insurance provider: ....

Where to find my insurance card: ....

....

....

My primary care doctor is: ....

His or her phone number is: ....

My preferred hospital for treatment is: ....

....

My preferred pharmacy for prescription fulfillment is: ....

....

....

If I Am Temporarily Incapacitated/Hospitalized...

Who needs to be contacted? ....

....

Any pets or plant care to note? ....

....

....

....

....

....

Important Contacts

Attorney name: ....

Phone number: ....

Executor name: ....

Phone number: ....

Accountant: ....

Phone number: ....

Health insurance agent: ....

Phone number: ....

Pastor, clergyman, or trusted advisor: ....

Phone number: ....

Point of Contact for Shareholders:

....

Phone Number: ....

Other important contact: ....

....

Relationship: ....

Phone Number: ....

Other important contact: ....

....

Relationship: ....

Phone Number: ....

Other important contact: ....

....

Relationship: ....

Phone Number: ....

Notes:

....

....

....

PART THREE

FINANCES

This section covers all things related to my personal and household finances, including bank account information and my financial power of attorney. For details on bills and autopay arrangements, see Part Five.

Power of Attorney

Where you can find my financial power of attorney document:
....

....

....

Checking Account Name and Number:
....

....

Bank Where Account is Located:
....

Online account username and password:
....

Checking Account Name and Number:
....

....

Bank Where Account is Located:
....

Online account username and password:
....

Savings Account Name and Number:
....

....

Bank Where Account is Located:
....

Online account username and password:
....

Savings Account Name and Number:
....

....

Bank Where Account is Located:
....

Online account username and password:
....

Misc. Account Name, Type, and Number:
....

....

Bank Where Account is Located:
....

Online account username and password:
....

Misc. Account Name, Type, and Number:
....

....

Bank Where Account is Located:
....

Online account username and password:
....

Misc. Account Name, Type, and Number:
....

....

Bank Where Account is Located:
....

Online account username and password:
....

CARDS

ATM card number:
....

Account Number:
....

Bank:
....

PIN:
....

Debit card number:
....

Account Number:
....

Bank:
....

PIN ....

Credit Card Company (example: MasterCard, Visa, etc.): ....

Account number: ....

Company phone number: ....

Online username and password: ....

Relevant misc. information regarding this card: ....

....

Credit Card Company (example: MasterCard, Visa, etc.): ....

Account number: ....

Company phone number: ....

Online username and password: ....

Relevant misc. information regarding this card: ....

....

Credit Card Company (example: MasterCard, Visa, etc.): ....

Account number: ....

Company phone number: ....

Online username and password: ....

Relevant misc. information regarding this card: ....

....

....

Store credit card: ....

Account Number: ....

Company's Credit Department Phone Number: ....

....

Store credit card: ....

Account Number: ....

Company's Credit Department Phone Number: ....

....

Store credit card: ....

Account Number: ....

Company's Credit Department Phone Number: ....

....

Store credit card: ....

Account Number: ....

Company's Credit Department Phone Number: ....

....

Notes: ....

....

....

....

STOCKS AND OTHER INVESTMENTS

Type of Investment: ....

....

Account number: ....

Who to Contact Regarding this Investment: ....

Misc. Notes on this Investment: ....

....

....

Type of Investment: ....

....

Account number: ....

Who to Contact Regarding this Investment: ....

Misc. Notes on this Investment: ....

....

....

Type of Investment: ....

....

Account number: ....

Who to Contact Regarding this Investment: ....

Misc. Notes on this Investment: ....

....

....

Type of Investment: ....

....

Account number: ....

Who to Contact Regarding this Investment: ....

Misc. Notes on this Investment: ....

....

....

Type of Investment: ....

....

Account number: ....

Who to Contact Regarding this Investment: ....

Misc. Notes on this Investment: ....

....

Type of Investment: ....

....

Account number: ....

Who to Contact Regarding this Investment: ....

Misc. Notes on this Investment: ....

....

....

Notes on Miscellaneous Accounts, such as Rewards Programs:
....

....

....

....

....

....

....

....

....

....

TAXES

Federal Records Location:
....

....

State Records Location:
....

....

Online tax account:
....

Username and password:
....

BUSINESS DETAILS

My business name is:
....
....
....

Address:
....
....

Who will act as temporary owner and operate if I am incapacitated and/or unable to communicate:
....
....

Upon my death, ownership of the company will be transferred to:
....
....
....

Important documents, licenses, and insurance policies for the business can be found:
....
....
....
....
....

Other information:

....

....

....

My business name is: ....

....

....

Address: ....

....

Who will act as temporary owner and operate if I am incapacitated and/or unable to communicate:

....

....

Upon my death, ownership of the company will be transferred to: ....

....

....

Important documents, licenses, and insurance policies for the business can be found: ....

....

....

....

....

....

....

Other information:
....

....

....

....

SAFE DEPOSIT BOXES

Bank Name:
....

....

Location of Branch Where Box is Located:
....

....

Number:
....

Where to Find the Key:
....

....

What's in the Box:
....

....

....

....

Misc. Notes: ....

....

....

....

Bank Name: ....

Location of Branch Where Box is Located: ....

....

....

Number: ....

Where to Find the Key: ....

....

What's in the Box: ....

....

....

....

Misc. Notes: ....

....

....

....

BILLS I AM RESPONSIBLE FOR AND LOAN THAT I OWE

Note: Please check with a lawyer and individual lenders as to which bills and payments carry over to the surviving and relevant beneficiary, and which are forgiven/no longer applicable after my passing.

Mortgage Lender: ....

Company phone number: ....

Account number: ....

Where to find relevant documents for this account: ....

....

....

....

Property taxes information: ....

....

....

....

Home Loan Lender: ....

Company phone number: ....

Account number: ....

Where to find relevant documents for this account: ....

....

....

....

Car Loan Lender: ....

Company phone number: ....

Account number: ....

Where to find relevant documents for this account: ....

....

....

Car Loan Lender: ....

Company phone number: ....

Account number: ....

Where to find relevant documents for this account: ....

....

....

Student Loan Lender: ....

Company phone number: ....

Account number: ....

Where to find relevant documents for this account: ....

....

....

....

Student Loan Lender: ....

Company phone number: ....

Account number: ....

Where to find relevant documents for this account: ....

....

....

....

Student Loan Lender: ....

Company phone number: ....

Account number: ....

Where to find relevant documents for this account: ....

....

....

....

Medical bills: ....

Company phone number: ....

Account number: ....

Where to find relevant documents for this account:

....

....

....

....

Description of service:

....

....

Collections history, if applicable:

....

....

....

....

....

Medical bills:

Company phone number:

Account number:

Where to find relevant documents for this account:

....

....

....

Description of service:
....
....
....

Collections history, if applicable:
....
....
....
....
....

Medical bills:
....

Company phone number:
....

Account number:
....

Where to find relevant documents for this account:
....
....
....

Description of service:
....
....
....

Collections history, if applicable:

....

....

....

....

....

....

Credit card: ....

Company phone number: ....

Account number: ....

Where to find relevant documents for this account: ....

....

....

....

Credit card: ....

Company phone number: ....

Account number: ....

Where to find relevant documents for this account: ....

....

....

....

Personal loan lender: ....

Company phone number: ....

Account number: ....

Where to find relevant documents for this account: ....

....

....

....

Personal loan lender: ....

Company phone number: ....

Account number: ....

Where to find relevant documents for this account: ....

....

....

....

Misc. Account: ....

Company phone number: ....

Account number: ....

Where to find relevant documents for this account: ....

....

....

Notes: ....

....

....

Misc. Account: ....

Company phone number: ....

Account number: ....

Where to find relevant documents for this account: ....

....

....

....

Notes: ....

....

....

....

....

....

....

....

....

PART FOUR

PROPERTY

In this section, you'll find information and guidance on personal and commercial properties I owned, as well as instructions for the sale or dispersal of my personal effects, including valuables and family heirlooms or sentimental objects. Some of these may also be covered in my will.

FOR THE OWNER OF THIS PLANNER: try to ensure that both your planner and will are consistent and up-to-date, as information included in your will is a legally written instruction; this planner is not. Example: if your will states a vintage car is to be given to your brother, but your planner indicates it should go to your son, the instruction written in the will is the legal one - even if it is not up-to-date.

REAL ESTATE

If You Own

Most recent physical residence (if multiple exist, use the one you spend the most time in):

....

....

....

....

....

Co-owner(s) of this property:

....

....

....

Where to find the keys:

....

....

Where to find the legal documents/deeds:

....

....

Warranty information and locations:

....

Landscaping and other service contracts can be found:

....

....

....

....

....

Home security company and number:

....

Misc. Notes on this property:

....

....

....

....

....

If You Rent

Rental address:

....

....

Where to find the lease:

....

Where to find the keys: ....

....

....

Lease expiration date: ....

Leasing office location and phone number: ....

....

Property manager name and phone number: ....

....

Misc. Notes on this rental: ....

....

....

....

....

Second Home or Residence (for personal use)

Description (example: land parcel, condominium, apartment, etc.): ....

....

....

....

....

....

....

....

Address:
....

....

Co-owner(s) of this property:
....

....

....

....

....

Where to find the keys:
....

....

Where to find the legal documents/deeds:
....

....

Warranty information and locations:
....

....

....

Misc. Notes on this property:

....
....
....
....
....
....
....

Commercial Property Description: ....

....
....
....
....

Co-owner(s) of this property: ....

....
....
....
....
....
....

Address:
....

....

Where to find the keys:
....

....

Where to find the legal documents, including current lease information:
....

....

....

Maintenance contract information (company name, number, service provided, and contract location in your files):
....

....

....

....

....

....

Misc. Notes on this property:
....

....

....

Commercial Property

Description: ....

....

....

....

....

Co-owner(s) of this property: ....

....

....

....

....

....

Address: ....

....

Where to find the keys: ....

....

Where to find the legal documents, including current lease information: ....

....

....

Maintenance contract information (company name, number, service provided, and contract location in your files):

....

....

....

....

....

....

....

Misc. Notes on this property:
....

....

....

....

Commercial Property Description:
....

....

....

....

Co-owner(s) of this property:
....

....

....

....

....

....

....

Address: ....

....

Where to find the keys: ....

....

Where to find the legal documents, including current lease information: ....

....

....

....

Maintenance contract information (company name, number, service provided, and contract location in your files):

....

....

....

....

....

Misc. Notes on this property:

VEHICLES AND RELATED ITEMS

Vehicle Type ((boat, trailer, RV, car, etc.):

Vehicle Year, Make and Model:

Vehicle Color:

Vehicle Identification Number:

Title Number:

Where to find the title:

Where to find the lease or loan document, if applicable:

Where to find the keys (main, backup, and valet sets, as needed):

....

....

....

Vehicle Type ((boat, trailer, RV, car, etc.):

....

Vehicle Year, Make and Model:

....

....

Vehicle Color:

Vehicle Identification Number:

Title Number:

Where to find the title:

....

Where to find the lease or loan document, if applicable:

....

Where to find the keys (main, backup, and valet sets, as needed):

....

....

....

Vehicle Type ((boat, trailer, RV, car, etc.):

....

Vehicle Year, Make and Model:

....

....

Vehicle Color:

Vehicle Identification Number:

Title Number:

Where to find the title:

....

Where to find the lease or loan document, if applicable:

....

....

Where to find the keys (main, backup, and valet sets, as needed):

....

....

....

Vehicle Type ((boat, trailer, RV, car, etc.):

....

Vehicle Year, Make and Model:

Vehicle Color: ....

Vehicle Identification Number: ....

Title Number: ....

Where to find the title: ....

....

Where to find the lease or loan document, if applicable: ....

....

Where to find the keys (main, backup, and valet sets, as needed): ....

....

....

....

Notes: ....

....

....

....

....

....

....

....

PERSONAL EFFECTS, SENTIMENTAL ITEMS, COLLECTIBLES, AND HEIRLOOMS

Item description:
....

....

....

Appraised value, if applicable:
....

....

Where to find it:
....

....

....

Is there a specific person I would like to receive this item?
....

....

....

Is there a story behind this item I would like to share?
....

....

....

....

Misc. notes regarding this item:
....

....

Item description: ....

....

....

Appraised value, if applicable: ....

....

Where to find it: ....

....

....

Is there a specific person I would like to receive this item? ....

....

....

Is there a story behind this item I would like to share? ....

....

....

....

....

Misc. notes regarding this item: ....

....

....

Item description: ....

....

....

Appraised value, if applicable: ....

....

Where to find it: ....

....

....

Is there a specific person I would like to receive this item? ....

....

....

Is there a story behind this item I would like to share? ....

....

....

....

....

Misc. notes regarding this item: ....

....

....

Item description:
....
....
....

Appraised value, if applicable:
....

Where to find it:
....
....

Is there a specific person I would like to receive this item?
....
....

Is there a story behind this item I would like to share?
....
....
....
....

Misc. notes regarding this item:
....
....

Item description: ....

....

....

Appraised value, if applicable: ....

....

Where to find it: ....

....

....

Is there a specific person I would like to receive this item? ....

....

....

Is there a story behind this item I would like to share? ....

....

....

....

....

Misc. notes regarding this item: ....

....

....

Item description: ....

....

....

Appraised value, if applicable: ....

....

Where to find it: ....

....

....

Is there a specific person I would like to receive this item? ....

....

....

Is there a story behind this item I would like to share? ....

....

....

....

....

Misc. notes regarding this item: ....

....

....

Item description:
....
....
....

Appraised value, if applicable:
....

Where to find it:
....
....

Is there a specific person I would like to receive this item?
....
....

Is there a story behind this item I would like to share?
....
....
....
....

Misc. notes regarding this item:
....
....

Item description: ....

....

....

Appraised value, if applicable: ....

....

Where to find it: ....

....

....

Is there a specific person I would like to receive this item? ....

....

....

Is there a story behind this item I would like to share? ....

....

....

....

....

Misc. notes regarding this item: ....

....

....

FIREARMS

Description (firearm type):
....
....
....
....

Registration information:
....
....
....

Permit:
....
....

Notes (include any relevant information regarding the firearm's use, history, and who you would like to receive it, if anyone):
....
....
....
....
....
....
....

Description (firearm type):

....

....

....

....

Registration information: ....

....

....

Permit: ....

....

Notes (include any relevant information regarding the firearm's use, history, and who you would like to receive it, if anyone):

....

....

....

....

....

....

....

Description (firearm type):

....

....

....

....

Registration information:

....

....

Permit:

....

....

Notes (include any relevant information regarding the firearm's use, history, and who you would like to receive it, if anyone):

....

....

....

....

....

....

....

....

Description (firearm type):

....

....

....

....

Registration information:

....

....

Permit:

....

....

Notes (include any relevant information regarding the firearm's use, history, and who you would like to receive it, if anyone):

....

....

....

....

....

....

....

Description (firearm type):

....

....

....

....

Registration information:

....

....

Permit:

....

....

Notes (include any relevant information regarding the firearm's use, history, and who you would like to receive it, if anyone):

....

....

....

....

....

....

....

NRA

NRA Membership? Circle one: Yes   No
....

NRA Member Number:
....

Card is located:
....

....

....

Notes:
....

....

....

....

....

....

....

....

....

....

....

....

SAFES

Physical description of safe:
....
....
....

Where to find the safe:
....
....
....

Where to find the keys, if applicable:
....
....
....

Combination:
....

Physical description of safe:
....
....
....

Where to find the safe:
....
....
....

Where to find the keys, if applicable:
....
....

Combination:
....

Physical description of safe: ....

....

....

Where to find the safe: ....

....

....

Where to find the keys, if applicable: ....

....

....

Combination: ....

STORAGE UNITS

Storage Company name and address: ....

....

....

Company phone number: ....

Unit number: ....

Gate code (if applicable): ....

Where to find the key(s): ....

....

Contents of Unit: ....

....

....

....

....

Misc. Notes regarding this unit:
....

....

Storage Company name and address:
....

....

....

Company phone number:
....

Unit number:
....

Gate code (if applicable):
....

Where to find the key(s):
....

....

Contents of Unit:
....

....

....

....

Misc. Notes regarding this unit: ....
....
....

Storage Company name and address: ....

....

....

Company phone number: ....

Unit number: ....

Gate code (if applicable): ....

Where to find the key(s): ....

....

Contents of Unit: ....

....

....

....

Misc. Notes regarding this unit: ....

....

....

....

Miscellaneous Objects and Hidden Valuables

Do I have any important objects and collectibles not listed above? Circle one: Yes   No

If "Yes" is Circled: What are the objects?

....

....

....

....

....

....

....

Where are they located?

....

....

....

Any special instructions or information related to these items?

....

....

....

....

Are any objects hidden for safekeeping? Where and what are they?

Have the items been appraised? Circle one: Yes   No

If "Yes," when was the most recent appraisal?

What was the estimated value of the item(s)?

Miscellaneous Notes on Part Four (Property)

PART FIVE

RECURRING BILLS OR AUTOPAYS

In this section, you will find a complete list of all the automatic and recurring payments in my name and/or linked to accounts in my name. These accounts should be moved to a relevant payment account or cancelled, as applicable.

For information regarding credit cards, please consult Part Three.

UTILITIES, PHONES, AND CABLE/INTERNET

Gas/oil company: ....

Phone number: ....

Water company: ....

Phone number: ....

Electricity: ....

Phone number: ....

Landline phone company: ....

Company phone number: ....

Mobile phone(s): ....

Providers: ....

....

Cable company: ....

Phone Number: ....

Internet provider - same as above? Circle one: Yes   No ....

If "No," specify provider: ....

Phone Number: ....

Notes: ....

....

....

CHARITIES I DONATE TO

Charity Name:
....

Charity Phone Number:
....

Is this a recurring donation (automatically drafted from account)? Circle one: Yes   No

If "Yes," on which bank account does this charge occur?
....

....

When does this charge occur?
....

What is the amount?
....

Charity Name:
....

Charity Phone Number:
....

Is this a recurring donation (automatically drafted from account)? Circle one: Yes   No

If "Yes," on which bank account does this charge occur?
....

....

When does this charge occur?
....

What is the amount?
....

Notes:
....

....

....

....

ONLINE RETAILERS (SUCH AS AMAZON PRIME)

Company: ....

Account number, if applicable: ....

Username and password: ....

Company: ....

Account number, if applicable: ....

Username and password: ....

Company: ....

Account number, if applicable: ....

Username and password: ....

MAGAZINE SUBSCRIPTIONS

Publication: ....

Subscription department phone number: ....

Address this publication is delivered to: ....

....

Automatic renewal? Circle one: Yes   No

If "Yes," on which account does this charge occur? ....

When will this charge occur? ....

Amount that will be charged: ....

Annual renewal, semi-annual, or other? Please specify. ....

....

....

....

....

....

Publication:
....

Subscription department phone number:
....

Address this publication is delivered to:
....

....

Automatic renewal? Circle one: Yes   No
....

If "Yes," on which account does this charge occur?
....

When will this charge occur?
....

Amount that will be charged:
....

Annual renewal, semi-annual, or other? Please specify.
....

....

....

....

....

Publication: ....

Subscription department phone number: ....

Address this publication is delivered to: ....

....

Automatic renewal? Circle one: Yes   No
....

If "Yes," on which account does this charge occur? ....

When will this charge occur? ....

Amount that will be charged: ....

Annual renewal, semi-annual, or other? Please specify. ....

....

....

....

....

....

LIBRARY CARD

My library: ....

My account/card number: ....

PIN for online use (note: if you have not chosen a PIN, it may be the last four of your social or the last four digits of your card number):
....

Library phone number: ....

Where to find my library card: ....

....

....

OTHER AUTOPAY ACCOUNTS (NETFLIX, HULU, GYM MEMBERSHIP, ETC.)

Company: ....

....

Username and password, if applicable: ....

Date of automatic charge: ....

Amount charged: ....

Frequency (monthly, yearly, etc.): ....

Bank account tied to this service: ....

Company: ....

....

Username and password, if applicable: ....

Date of automatic charge: ....

Amount charged: ....

Frequency (monthly, yearly, etc.): ....

Bank account tied to this service: ....

....

Company: ....

....

Username and password, if applicable: ....

Date of automatic charge: ....

Amount charged: ....

Frequency (monthly, yearly, etc.): ....

Bank account tied to this service: ....

....

MISCELLANEOUS NOTES ON ONLINE PAYMENT ACCOUNTS AND AUTOPAY ARRANGEMENTS:

....

....

....

....

....

....

....

....

....

PART SIX

ODDS AND ENDS

In this section, you find all the information on my email, social media accounts, and other online log-ins, as well as my wishes for each account. I've also included who should know about this planner after my death, who already knows about it, and what I would like to happen in the event I become incapacitated or otherwise unable to communicate.

(FOR THE OWNER OF THIS PLANNER: consult the Terms of Service for each website's rules and protocols when a user passes. It's also a good idea to save personal items stored in these accounts—such as photos—to an external hard drive or USB drive, and/or print hard copies for safekeeping. Be sure to update this section as your log-in emails and passwords change.)

EMAIL

Provider: ....

Username/address ....

Password: ....

I would like this account... Circle one: Closed   Left   Open ....

If you circled "Left Open," specify why, who is allowed to access it, and when you would like it closed:

....

....

....

....

Provider: ....

Username/address ....

Password: ....

I would like this account... Circle one: Closed   Left   Open ....

If you circled "Left Open," specify why, who is allowed to access it, and when you would like it closed:

....

....

....

....

Provider:
....

Username/address
....

Password:
....

I would like this account... Circle one: Closed   Left   Open
....

If you circled "Left Open," specify why, who is allowed to access it, and when you would like it closed:

....

....

....

....

....

Provider:
....

Username/address
....

Password:
....

I would like this account... Circle one: Closed   Left   Open
....

If you circled "Left Open," specify why, who is allowed to access it, and when you would like it closed:

....

....

....

....

....

SOCIAL MEDIA

Facebook: ....

Username/profile URL: ....

Password: ....

I would like this account... Circle one: Closed   Left   Open

If you circled "Left Open," specify why, who is allowed to access it, and when you would like it closed:

....

....

....

....

Twitter: ....

Username/Handle: ....

Password: ....

I would like this account... Circle one: Closed   Left   Open

If you circled "Left Open," specify why, who is allowed to access it, and when you would like it closed:

....

....

....

....

Instagram: ....

Username: ....

Password: ....

I would like this account... Circle one: Closed   Left   Open ....

If you circled "Left Open," specify why, who is allowed to access it, and when you would like it closed:

....

....

....

....

....

LinkedIn: ....

Profile URL: ....

Password: ....

I would like this account... Circle one: Closed   Left   Open ....

If you circled "Left Open," specify why, who is allowed to access it, and when you would like it closed:

....

....

....

....

....

Pinterest: ....

Profile URL: ....

Password: ....

I would like this account... Circle one:　　Closed　　　Left　　　Open

If you circled "Left Open," specify why, who is allowed to access it, and when you would like it closed:

....

....

....

....

Other: ....

Profile URL: ....

Password: ....

I would like this account... Circle one:　　Closed　　　Left　　　Open

If you circled "Left Open," specify why, who is allowed to access it, and when you would like it closed:

....

....

....

....

Other: ....

Profile URL: ....

Password: ....

I would like this account... Circle one: Closed   Left   Open ....

If you circled "Left Open," specify why, who is allowed to access it, and when you would like it closed:

....

....

....

....

Other: ....

Profile URL: ....

Password: ....

I would like this account... Circle one: Closed   Left   Open ....

If you circled "Left Open," specify why, who is allowed to access it, and when you would like it closed:

....

....

....

....

PERSONAL WEBSITES OR BLOGS

Web address: ....

Username and password: ....

Administrator name and phone number: ....

Domain host: ....

I would like this account... Circle one: Closed   Left   Open ....

If you circled "Left Open," specify why, who is allowed to access it, and when you would like it closed:

....

....

....

....

....

Misc. Notes on this webpage: ....

....

....

....

....

....

....

Web address: ....

Username and password: ....

Administrator name and phone number: ....

Domain host: ....

I would like this account... Circle one: Closed   Left   Open ....

If you circled "Left Open," specify why, who is allowed to access it, and when you would like it closed:

....

....

....

....

....

Misc. Notes on this webpage: ....

....

....

....

....

....

....

Web address: ....

Username and password: ....

Administrator name and phone number: ....

Domain host: ....

I would like this account... Circle one: Closed   Left   Open ....

If you circled "Left Open," specify why, who is allowed to access it, and when you would like it closed:

....

....

....

....

....

Misc. Notes on this webpage: ....

....

....

....

....

....

....

....

BUSINESS WEBSITES OR BLOGS

Web address: ....

Username and password: ....

Administrator name and phone number: ....

Domain host: ....

I would like this account... Circle one: Closed   Left   Open

If you circled "Left Open," specify why, who is allowed to access it, and when you would like it closed:

....

....

....

....

....

Misc. Notes on this webpage:

....

....

....

....

....

....

Web address: ....

Username and password: ....

Administrator name and phone number: ....

Domain host: ....

I would like this account... Circle one: Closed   Left   Open ....

If you circled "Left Open," specify why, who is allowed to access it, and when you would like it closed:

....

....

....

....

....

Misc. Notes on this webpage: ....

....

....

....

....

....

....

....

PASSWORDS AND PASSCODES

Internet Router Location in Home:

Login and password:

Internet Router Location in Commercial Property:

Login and password:

Internet Router Location in Secondary or Vacation Residence:

Login and password:

Home Security System Provider (Home):

Passcode:

Security Provider for Commercial Property:

Passcode:

Security Provider for Commercial Property:

Passcode:

Security Provider for Commercial Property:

Passcode:

Security Provider for Secondary or Vacation Residence

Passcode:

Notes:

COMPUTER, PHONE, AND TABLET PASSWORDS

Device: ....

Passcode: ....

Device: ....

Passcode: ....

Device: ....

Passcode: ....

Device: ....

Passcode: ....

Device: ....

Passcode: ....

Notes: ....

....

....

....

....

....

....

....

IN THE EVENT I AM ALIVE BUT UNABLE TO COMMUNICATE, I WOULD LIKE MY CAREGIVERS TO KNOW...

(To the owner of this planner: please provide any instructions or wishes you'd like your caregivers and family members to know. This can include care preferences, hospital preferences, and who will make decisions on your behalf.)

....

....

....

....

....

....

....

....

....

....

....

....

....

....

....

....

WHO KNOWS ABOUT MY PLANNER?

The following people know about this planner's existence; some may know its location and/or already know its contents. This is specified under each person's name and contact information.

Name:

Relationship:

Phone Number:

Address:

Do they know where this planner is located? Circle one: Yes   No

Have they read this planner, or parts of it? Circle one: Yes   No

Would I like them to read it in its entirety, or a specific section?

Name:

Relationship:

Phone Number:

Address:

Do they know where this planner is located? Circle one: Yes   No

Have they read this planner, or parts of it? Circle one: Yes   No

Would I like them to read it in its entirety, or a specific section?

Name: ....

Relationship: ....

Phone Number: ....

Address: ....

Do they know where this planner is located? Circle one: Yes   No

Have they read this planner, or parts of it? Circle one: Yes   No

Would I like them to read it in its entirety, or a specific section?

....

....

....

Name: ....

Relationship: ....

Phone Number: ....

Address: ....

Do they know where this planner is located? Circle one: Yes   No

Have they read this planner, or parts of it? Circle one: Yes   No

Would I like them to read it in its entirety, or a specific section?

....

....

....

Name: ....

Relationship: ....

Phone Number: ....

Address: ....

Do they know where this planner is located? Circle one: Yes   No

Have they read this planner, or parts of it? Circle one: Yes   No

Would I like them to read it in its entirety, or a specific section?

....

....

....

Name: ....

Relationship: ....

Phone Number: ....

Address: ....

Do they know where this planner is located? Circle one: Yes   No

Have they read this planner, or parts of it? Circle one: Yes   No

Would I like them to read it in its entirety, or a specific section?

....

....

....

Name: ....

Relationship: ....

Phone Number: ....

Address: ....

Do they know where this planner is located? Circle one: Yes   No ....

Have they read this planner, or parts of it? Circle one: Yes   No ....

Would I like them to read it in its entirety, or a specific section? ....

....

....

....

Name: ....

Relationship: ....

Phone Number: ....

Address: ....

Do they know where this planner is located? Circle one: Yes   No ....

Have they read this planner, or parts of it? Circle one: Yes   No ....

Would I like them to read it in its entirety, or a specific section? ....

....

....

....

MISCELLANEOUS NOTES (WHO IS ABSOLUTELY NOT ALLOWED TO READ THIS PLANNER, IF ANYONE? DO I WANT PHOTOCOPIES MADE FOR CERTAIN FAMILY MEMBERS OR FRIENDS AFTER MY PASSING?):

....

....

....

....

....

....

....

....

....

....

....

....

....

....

....

....

....

PART SEVEN

PARTING WORDS

This section includes any final thoughts regarding my estate, funerary services, or medical care that I did not think to include before, or that did not fit into the previous sections.
I'll also use this section for my final words to my loved ones and friends, or describe where to find letters already written for this purpose.

(TO THE OWNER OF THIS PLANNER: this is where you can write goodbyes, fun memories, and personalized messages to the family members or friends who will read this planner after you pass. Don't feel overwhelmed--you don't have to include everything and everyone, if you don't want to. Some poems, verses from the Bible or other religious texts, or comforting messages you think your loved ones will enjoy are great to include. Think of what you would like to read in the event you lost that loved one--what would bring you comfort or peace, during such a difficult time?)

Made in the USA
Monee, IL
13 September 2020